Contents

Left: Completed in 2010, a new temple beside That Luang in Vientiane.

Above right: A carved door panel at Vat Xieng Thong, one of Luang Prabang's most beautiful and historic temples.

Below right: A colourful vehicle known locally as a 'jumbo' whisks through the centre of Luang Prabang.

Chapter 1: Mystery and Intrigue

Few countries conjure up such a sense of mystery and intrigue in the traveller's mind as mountainous, landlocked Laos. Regarded as Southeast Asia's sleepy backwater, for many years Laos' communist government ensured that the country remained closed to the outside world. Unconcerned by neighbouring Thailand's dash for modernity, Laos resolutely moved at its own pace. When the door was finally eased open for travellers in the early 90s, it revealed a beautiful country with a fascinating culture and an ethnically diverse population.

Today, Laos is well and truly awakening from its slumber. The capital, Vientiane (pronounced Vien-chan) bustles with renewed energy and is benefiting from considerable Chinese and Korean investment. In the vibrant city, with its new-found wealth, an abundance of shining SUVs and an emerging middle class, it's hard to believe you are in one of Asia's poorest nations. Many of Laos' attractions, however, lie beyond the capital. Here, the rural population still ekes out an existence as subsistence farmers, fishermen, market traders and merchants. For many in the countryside, little has changed. That in itself is part of Laos' enduring appeal for visitors.

Above: Boat trips down the Mekong River add a new perspective to travel in Laos.

Left: A young girl runs past a colonial-era building in the southern town of Pakse.

Opposite above: A small golden Buddha image outside a temple in Luang Prabang.

Opposite below: Linten girls, one of the many ethnic hill tribe groups in northern Laos.

Rich Cultural Heritage

Laos is a destination for the true cultural traveller. The country's greatest asset, apart from the genuinely warm and welcoming population of just over 6 million citizens, is its rich culture and stunning natural beauty. In the north, the splendours of the UNESCO World Heritage town of Luang Prabang attract thousands of visitors each year who enjoy relaxed days wandering streets lined with colonial-era French architecture and discovering ancient temples, and languid evenings of alfresco dining beside the turbulent

Opposite: Old wooden Buddha images at Vat Xieng Thong, Luang Prabang.

Opposite below right: A group of monks heading back to the temple in a minibus.

Below: The entranceways to Lao temples are always beautifully decorated.

waters of the Mekong River. Further north, Luang Nam Tha, a mountainous forested land and home to the country's many hill tribes, attracts trekkers and nature lovers. On the outskirts of Phonsavan, rolling hills are scattered with mysterious stone jars that still manage to confound archaeologists. Equally hard to fathom is the fact that the sparsely populated landscape also bears the scars of the world's heaviest aerial bombardment and a deadly legacy of American unexploded ordnance. Southeast of Vientiane, the rugged province of Khammouane is emerging as another eco-travel hotspot, while in the far south, Champasak Province is home to the UNESCO World Heritage Site of Vat Phou, a magnificent 1,000-year-old temple ruin that is testament to a glorious past. Travelling still further south, the mighty Mekong has devoured the landscape to create a unique region known as Si Pan Don, or 4,000 Islands, before it spills over the border into Cambodia.

Whether exploring the rich cultural heritage, engaging with colourful hill tribes or enjoying a leisurely cruise down the Mekong River, laidback, landlocked Laos never fails to inspire and enchant.

Geography and Climate

Bordered by China, Myanmar, Thailand, Cambodia and Vietnam, tiny Laos encompasses 236,800 square kilometres (91,425 square miles). Laos is an elongated country divided into 18 provinces. Seventy-five per cent of the country is mountainous with a total of 40 per cent forest cover, although this is rapidly being removed by legal and illegal logging and the construction of hydroelectric dams.

Laos' fertile floodplains, lush valleys and hillsides have been sculpted by irrigation channels and rice paddies. Here, seasons are marked by the colours of burnt sienna when the soil is tilled, the brilliant green of gently swaying young rice plants and tones of yellow ochre at harvest time.

Some of the country's most rugged and dramatic landscapes are found in the north. Here, the forested terrain can reach 2,800 m (9,190 ft). Despite the logging and a seemingly uncontrolled trade in endangered wildlife, Laos is still home to many rare plants and animals. On the country's eastern border, the long chain of the Annamite Mountains rises in places to 2,500 m (8,200 ft). In the valleys of the north and east, the mainly agrarian population grows rice and other cash-crops, such as sweetcorn, lettuce and a wide variety of herbs.

In central Laos, the land around Vientiane is used for rice production and other crops. The area is also known for the Nam Ngum Reservoir, which borders Phou Khao Khouay, one of the country's 27 national parks and areas of biodiversity conservation.

In the southeast, the 1,300-m (4,265-ft) Bolaven Plateau enjoys a cooler micro-climate. On the plateau, the area around the town of Pakxong is the centre of Laos' arabica coffee industry. Visitors to the area enjoy beautiful scenery, national parks, cascading waterfalls and hill tribe villages.

In southern Laos, protected areas in parts of Champasak and Attapeu Provinces are home to Asian Elephants, Asiatic Black Bears, gibbons, tigers and the highest recorded number of Laos' bird species. Further south, the intriguing landscape of Si Pan Don attracts travellers, many of whom come to try and glimpse the endangered Irrawaddy Dolphin in the waters of the Mekong Delta.

Laos enjoys a tropical climate with average high temperatures of 35°C (95°F). There are three overlapping seasons. The monsoon lasts from May to October followed by the cool season which runs until February. During this period, it can be extremely fresh and cold in the evenings and early mornings, particularly in the north but usually warms up during the day. Temperatures and humidity begin to rise towards the end of February, with the peak of the hot season being in April.

Opposite left: Rice is still harvested by hand. The backbreaking work is often carried out by the whole family.

Opposite right: During the cool season, the waters of the Mekong recede and vegetables are planted in the fertile soil.

Above: The valleys of northern Laos are covered with rice paddies.

The Mekong

It's impossible to overestimate the importance of the Mekong River to the people of Laos. From its source in Tibet's Jifu Mountains, the Mekong enters the country in the northwestern province of Luang Nam Tha where the borders of China, Laos and Myanmar converge. The mighty river continues its journey the entire length of Laos, for much of the time forming a natural border with Thailand, before widening to almost 14 km (nearly nine miles) during the height of the rainy season at Si Pan Don, then flowing into Cambodia.

Above: *Fishermen on the Mekong checking their nets.*

Above: *During the hot season, navigation of the Mekong can be difficult as the water level drops considerably and rocks are exposed.*

Above: Mekong sunsets can be really dramatic. In many towns, riverside restaurants are the perfect place to end the day with a delicious meal and an ice-cold Beerlao.

Above: An incredible variety of fish is caught in the Mekong and sold fresh in the country's many morning markets.

Known in Lao as the *Mae Nahm Kong* (literally 'mother river'), the Mekong feeds the nation with a huge variety of freshwater fish, which along with rice grown on the massive fertile floodplain that runs from Xayabouri to Champasak, is the mainstay of the Lao diet. In the cool and dry seasons, its fertile banks and islands are planted with a wide variety of vegetables.

The Mekong is an essential trade route for goods from China and its many tributaries provide access to remote villages. The river is also still used in the Buddhist ceremonies that follow a cremation, carrying the ashes of the deceased in a simple earthenware jar to the bottom of its murky waters and on to the next life.

Yet despite the huge numbers of Laos' rural population who depend on the river for their livelihood, the Mekong and its bounty face an uncertain future. A series of hydroelectric dams constructed in the valleys for the export of energy brought a much needed inflow of money to the nation and earned it the nickname, the 'battery of Asia'. Now controversial dams at several locations on the Mekong are planned raising concerns about the environment.

A Brief History of Laos

Archaeological evidence of ancient ceramics and bronze artefacts reveals that Laos was inhabited by scattered settlements as long as 10,000 years ago. It is known that peoples began migrating into what is now Laos during the 8–10th century AD from southern China and northern Vietnam.

Above: *The former royal palace in Luang Prabang is now the National Museum.*

Laos' first recorded history, however, is in 1353 when King Fa Ngum ruled over Lan Xang, the 'land of a million elephants', from Muang Sawa, or what is now known as Luang Prabang. King Fa Ngum is also credited with making Theravada Buddhism the state religion. A warrior king, he is said to have taken possession of a golden Buddha image known as the Pha Bang from the Khmers, which prompted the city's name to be changed to Luang Pha Bang, meaning

Great Pha Bang. King Fa Ngum was succeeded by his son, Phaya Samsenthai who married two Thai princesses and ruled over a burgeoning state for 43 years. This relatively stable period of Lao history was followed by a century of turbulence and a dozen or more rulers.

In 1560, King Setthathirath moved the capital to Vientiane – then known as Wieng Chan – a change designed to diffuse increased aggression from neighbouring Myanmar.

During the reign of King Suriya Vongsa in the 17th century, Laos is said to have enjoyed a golden age and began attracting attention from Europe. Following King Suriya Vongsa's 57-year reign, the kingdom of Lan Xang was broken into three parts by a feudal power struggle, namely Luang Prabang, Wieng Chan and Champasak. Later in 1763, Luang Prabang was taken by Burmese armies and Champasak by the Siamese.

Above: Monks walk past a statue of King Sisavang Phoulivong. He is holding the Lao constitution in his right hand. Crowned in 1905, he reigned until his death in 1959.

Above right: Luang Prabang and the southern towns of Tha Kaek and Savannakhet have some particularly fine examples of French colonial buildings although many are now in need of restoration.

Colonial Rule

The Siamese went on to increase their power and by the end of the 18th century controlled Wieng Chan and Luang Prabang. However, the expansion of European dominance in the region saw the Siamese relinquish power to the French and in 1893 Laos became a colony of French Indochina. This was also the period in which Laos established its present-day national borders. Today many fabulous colonial-era buildings remain in Laos, although many are in a state of disrepair.

During the period of French colonial rule, Prince Souphanounvong sought out support from Vietnam for the formation of a Lao communist movement and in 1950 established Lao Issara, or the Free Laos Resistance, to fight and expel the French.

A Secret War

Laos gained independence in 1953 but suffered two decades of civil war including secret saturation bombing by the U.S. Air Force. During the Vietnam War, U.S. planes dropped more than two million tons of bombs over Laos—double the amount dropped over Germany during World War II. Between 1964 and 1973, the USA flew 580,000 bombing missions over Laos — one every nine minutes for ten years. On a per-capita basis, Laos remains the most heavily bombed nation in history. UXO units from the U.K. and Australia have been working in the country for years and continue to do so today, trying to clear the unexploded ordnance. Over 87,000 km² (33,590 sq miles) of land are considered as being at risk, rendering vast areas of farmland in this predominantly agrarian countryside unusable. There have also been 20,000 casualties due to UXO since 1974, many of them children, and 300 Laotians continue to be injured or die each year.

Above: The deadly legacy of unexploded bombs still claims many victims every year.

Raise the Red Flag – The Creation of Lao PDR

In 1975, the Pathet Lao mounted a coup d'état that deposed King Sisavang Vatthana and ended six centuries of royal rule. When the new Lao People's Democratic Republic was formed, some 300,000 lowland Lao royalists, around 10 per cent of the population at the time, fled the country. Many of these were middle-class businesspeople, skilled workers and civil servants, and it is clear that even today this loss of educated citizens continues to severely restrict the nation's social and political development.

Following the creation of Lao PDR (still the official name of Laos), the country suffered severe economic decline and political isolation to become one of the world's poorest nations. In the early 90s, the government slowly began to promote private enterprise and encourage foreign investment. Today, with large amounts of foreign aid as well as investment and income from the sale of hydroelectric power to Thailand, there is increased prosperity for connected individuals and the new middle class. Wealth is slow to trickle down, however, and the majority of Lao people remain in poverty.

Challenging Times Ahead

Following a period of rather frosty relations, perhaps thawed out by the prospect of cheap electricity from new hydroelectric dams, Thailand is now a large investor in Laos. In reality, and as a result of its period of relative isolation during a time when the rest of Southeast Asia was booming, Laos seems to have retained many of the endearing qualities and culture which Thailand has already lost or is in danger of losing.

Laos remains one of the world's last self-proclaimed socialist republics, although its socialist principles are hard to detect in modern-day Vientiane. In recent years, Vietnam

has become the largest investor in Laos, followed by China and Thailand. The Lao government has signed dozens of contracts with China including concessions for agribusiness industries, particularly rubber, timber, mining and telecoms. Thousands of Chinese migrants have also established themselves in northern Laos and Vientiane. This has caused many to express concern about the future of Laos' natural resources and question the wisdom of allowing such a huge influx of migrant labour to take root in the country. The future for Laos is indeed challenging.

This page: Just outside the town of Phonsavan there are several war memorials that commemorate the thousands of Pathet Lao soldiers who lost their lives during the Indochina Wars and to honour Vietnamese soldiers who fought alongside them.

The People

With a population of just 6,300,000 (2011), Laos has the lowest population density in Southeast Asia. The country is made up of a colourful mix of 68 different ethnic people but these are commonly divided into four main groups that refer to the altitude at which they live.

Below: Lao children in rural areas grow up happy and carefree.

These are the Lao Loum or lowland Lao who make up roughly 50% of the population; the Lao Tai or tribal Tai which includes the Tai Dam or black Tai; the Lao Theung or lower mountain people who are of Mon-Khmer decent; and the Lao Soong or the hill tribes who live at the greatest altitude. The highest concentration of hill tribes is in the far north in villages located above 1,000 m (3,280 ft). Most settled in Laos after migrating from southern China, Burma and Tibet early last century. Visitors to the northern towns of Muang Sing and Luang Nam Tha are likely to see different tribal peoples in the local markets including the Hmong, Akha, Yao, Lisu and Lahu, among many others.

Other Asians who have an established presence in Laos are the Chinese and Vietnamese. The Chinese have a long history of migration to Laos but in recent years there has been an influx of so-called temporary workers who come mainly from Yunnan province in southern China to work on construction projects. Most urban communities have a long-established and sizeable Vietnamese population, dating from the time of the French colonization when they came as aides and their entourage.

Left: A young Lao woman enjoying the fun at New Year.

Above left: Laos has a large population of Vietnamese, particularly in the capital Vientiane and the provinces bordering Vietnam.

Above: Most of Laos' many hill tribes live in the mountainous north of the country. Many still live in remote villages and survive by subsistence farming. Colourful traditional clothing distinguishes each tribe or sub-tribe, such as the Akha girl shown here.

Religion and Beliefs

Today, it is estimated that about 65–70% of Lao people are Theravada Buddhists. The religion plays an important role within Lao society and many poor children receive a basic education at temples.

Above: Many Lao Buddhists regularly attend the temple to make offerings of flowers, incense and food as well as donations of money. On special religious days, temples are often crowded with the faithful seeking the blessing of the monks.

Right: Large trees in Laos are often decorated and used as shrines for prayer and making offerings to the spirits. The plumeria tree, or 'don champa', is considered to be a sacred tree and is planted in the grounds of many temples.

Left: At Lao New Year, images of the Buddha are sprinkled with perfumed water and flowers. The washing of the images, of homes and of the feet of the elderly is associated with prosperity and longevity.

Below: The daily merit-making ritual of offering food to monks, known as 'tak bat', is still widely practised in Laos. Monks emerge from the temples at 5.30 a.m. and walk the streets collecting small donations of sticky rice.

Every Lao Buddhist man is expected to become a monk for a short period of his life. The usual period is for a minimum of three months. Serving in the monkhood is considered of great importance for the family of the young man. It is usually during Buddhist Lent or *phansaa* in the rainy season that new monks are initiated into the order. Young boys may become novices at any age but a man cannot become a fully fledged monk until he reaches the age of twenty. He can then remain a monk for as long as he wishes.

Right: A monk at Vat Si Muang in Vientiane performs a ritual to bless worshippers.

Opposite above: Many Lao people still use traditional medicine that is sold in local markets. A wide variety of remedies is available made from dried herbs, roots and animal parts.

Opposite below: A spirit house built to honour the dead in northern Laos by ethnic Tai Dam includes offerings of money, incense and food. Offerings to the spirits can also include cows' heads which are left to decay at the shrine.

The Spirit World

Animism is common within the tribal Tai groups and the hill tribes. Spirit houses outside homes, shrines to ancestors and totems placed at the entrance to villages to ward off evil are all part of Laos' fascinating spirit world.

Predating Buddhism, spirit worship believes that *phii* or spirits inhabit natural objects and the land. Spirit houses are placed outside homes and daily offerings made to placate the spirits. Many Lao also believe that 32 spirits known as *khwan* act as guardians of a person's mind and body. If the spirits leave the body, a person may become weak and susceptible to illness and danger. *Baasi*, a commonly performed ritual in which white threads are tied around the wrist, calls back any wayward spirits and binds them to the body. The ceremony is often performed as a welcome for guests, at births and weddings and before embarking on a long journey. Interestingly, this is one of many spirit rituals that have also become part of Buddhist worship and play a role in *boun pii mai* – the Lao New Year celebrations. In addition to the belief in the spirit world, some highland tribes, such as the Hmong and Akha, also practise ancestor worship.

Lao Food

It only takes a short time to realize that the nation marches – or in the case of Laos, strolls rather casually – on a diet whose main staple is rice. In common with northern and northeastern Thailand, the Lao eat mainly glutinous rice, a malleable steamed grain served at the table in woven baskets, although boiled fragrant rice is also eaten.

Also central to the Lao diet is a wide variety of freshwater fish which are steamed, grilled and fried, or made into a salad called *goy pla*. A fermented fish paste known as *pla daek* is used to flavour many dishes. Perhaps the most popular dish is *laap*, which is a mix of minced meat, tossed in lime juice, dried chillis, fish sauce and toasted rice powder and flavoured with herbs.

Above: A popular Lao dish is fish stuffed with herbs such as Lao basil and lemongrass, covered in salt and barbecued.

Right: Sticky rice is commonly eaten in Laos. The grain is steamed until it becomes soft and malleable.

Above: In Laos, cooked food to take home is sold in the morning and evening markets. Rich in vegetables and fish, the Lao diet is one of the healthiest in Asia.

Right: At the table, sticky rice is often served in small baskets. Farmers will also take baskets of sticky rice to the fields to eat for lunch with steamed vegetables and a spicy chilli dip known as 'nam phrik'.

Regional Cuisine and Colourful Markets

Although restaurant menus in Laos can be very limited in scope and increasingly draw upon versions of Thai dishes such as the spicy *tom yam* fish soup or *gaeng som*, a similar but slightly sour soup, regional favourites can be found in the local markets. In Luang Prabang, dishes include the delicious *aw laam*, a kind of vegetable stew thickened with broken sticky rice and gently spiced with the addition of pieces of *sakarn* wood, and *sin savan*, thin slices of sun-dried beef served with *jaew bong*, a roasted chilli paste. *Kaipen*, tasty sheets of dried river weed, similar to Japanese *nori*, are also a popular snack.

Further north in Luang Nam Tha, markets are particularly colourful due to the presence of many different ethnic groups such as the Tai Dam and Akha peoples. Sellers have a particularly endearing way of arranging their produce in small heaps or freshly cooked food in portion-sized bowls, ready to tip into a bag when a customer makes a purchase. The ladies take great care with their beautiful displays, bunching salad vegetables together and threading them on strips of bamboo and arranging small river fish in patterns. It's a visual feast.

Above: *Food vendors offer produce for sale in individual portions.*

Opposite: *A lady in the market arranges her produce which includes piles of ant eggs. A good source of protein, they are used in soups, curries and salads.*

Right: Wild food is enjoyed by many in Laos. These lizards will be grilled and served with a spicy mango salad.

Opposite above: Vietnamese dishes, such as 'ban cuan', steamed rice flour sheets stuffed with minced pork and mushrooms, are popular for breakfast enjoyed with strong coffee with condensed milk.

Opposite below: Despite the fact that Laos has now opened its market to other beers, Beerlao still reigns supreme and is the tipple of choice for the vast majority of drinkers, locals and tourists.

Wild Food

In rural areas travellers are likely to see a wide range of wildlife for sale in the fresh markets. To many, this can often be a disturbing sight especially when you consider the fragile nature of Laos' environment. However, many in rural Lao villages are very poor and most eke out a living as subsistence farmers. Wild food has always been an important part of the diet. Creatures ready for the pot to be seen on sale in markets include civet cat, squirrel, porcupine, jungle rats, a variety of wild birds, bats, frogs, tadpoles and snakes. Ant eggs are also added to soups, curries and salads, and fried insects, such as crickets, are a popular and nutritious snack.

Outside Influences

The culinary landscape of Laos is no less effected by its past than is its architecture or its politics. In the late 60s and 70s, during the Vietnam war, many Vietnamese sought refuge in Laos. Today, the culinary tradition that they brought with them is extremely popular. Vietnamese dishes include the ubiquitous *foe*, a comforting noodle soup of beef, buffalo, pork or chicken with liberal additions of fresh herbs and vegetables and, of course, fiery chillis. Other Vietnamese favourites include *naem neaung*, tasty little 'do-it-yourself' rice paper wraps filled with grilled pork balls, lettuce and herbs, *ban cuan*, steamed rice flour sheets stuffed with pork and mushrooms and *yor kao* and *yor jeun*, fresh and fried spring rolls.

Laotians also enthusiastically accepted the baguette when it was introduced during the French colonial period. In Vientiane, baguettes are sold on street corners and in the local markets but with a distinctly local twist. Warmed over a charcoal brazier, split down the middle, smeared with pâté and stuffed with pork, raw papaya, pickled vegetables and a lick of hot chilli sauce, the baguettes make a satisfying breakfast when served with thick, sweet Lao coffee.

The National Brew

One of the country's biggest exports and best selling products at home is Beerlao. The brew is regarded as one of the finest beers in Southeast Asia. You can't miss it; Beerlao has over 95 per cent of the local beer market, almost all restaurants have the distinctive green Beerlao signs outside and T-shirts with the logos abound. A few years ago, Carlsberg bought half of the company; one more sign of the economic success of the brand. Visitors to Vientiane can enjoy a tour of the brewery to be found on the outskirts of the city.

Festivals and Events

Laos' colourful festival calendar includes regular celebrations known locally as *boun*. Visitors are likely to come across *boun wat* and *het boun*, temple fairs and events held as part of a local celebration or day of thanks.

New Year Celebrations

In January or February, depending on the lunar calendar, the Chinese and Vietnamese communities mark their annual New Year celebrations with lion dances in the streets and feasting, particularly in downtown Vientiane. The Lao celebrate their New Year, *boun pii mai*, from April 13–16. People will visit many temples to take part in the ritual bathing of Buddha images in order to make merit. This is also a time for cleaning the house and washing the Buddha images at shrines within the home. Outside, increasingly boisterous water fights take place in the streets from dawn till dusk. Vientiane and Luang Prabang are regarded as the best places to see *boun pii mai*. The hill tribes welcome their own New Year, usually in January or February.

Makha Busa

One of Laos' most important annual Buddhist festivals is *makha busa*. The event commemorates two separate events that are said to have occurred on the same date during the Buddha's lifetime but 45 years apart; namely the coming together of 1,250 monks to be ordained by the Buddha and the Buddha delivering his teachings shortly before his death. Held during the full moon of the third lunar month, usually in February, the largest festival takes place at Vat Phou, the UNESCO World Heritage Site in Champasak Province. Hundreds of monks and Buddhist pilgrims gather at Vat Phou for three days of celebrations and merit-making. The nearby town of Champasak is inundated with visitors and it is impossible to find accommodation at this time. Many sleep out in the open under simple shelters close to the temple site.

Two other important festivals are *boun khao phansa* and *boun ok phansa*, which mark the beginning and end of Buddhist Lent, during which time all monks stay in their temples and believers bring supplies to them.

Above: 'Boun pii mai', Laos New Year, is celebrated all over the country with three days of boisterous water fights from dawn until dusk. New Year in Laos is also a time for cleaning the house and washing Buddha images at home and in the temples.

Left: As part of the 'boun pii mai' festivities, sand pagodas are built in the grounds of temples and on the banks of the Mekong River. It is believed that the grains of sand will keep the worshippers from sin. Visitors to the temple at New Year decorate the pagodas with colourful flags.

Right: At 'boun pii mai' devotees visit many temples and sprinkle the Buddha images with perfumed water and flower petals.

Opposite page: The annual rocket festival of 'boun bang fai'. Competing teams make powerful homemade rockets which are fired into the sky in the belief that they will ensure a good rainy season and a bountiful rice harvest.

Boun Bang Fai

Rainmaking rocket festivals, or *boun bang fai*, are held all over Laos in May and June. Several days before the actual celebrations begin, villagers gather together to mix gunpowder and make rockets of varying sizes. In the past, the explosive was pushed into bamboo tubes but today blue plastic drainage pipes are more common. The day of celebration begins with a village parade, dancing and music, followed by the launching of hugely powerful and decidedly dangerous rockets into the sky by competing teams. The rocket's fuse is lit using an electrical charge from a car battery and it can reach an incredible height. People believe the rockets will provoke the clouds into unleashing the season's rain and thereby produce a good rice harvest. Wooden phallic symbols are also commonly seen at the festival, a clear sign of the festival's connection to fertility.

Boun Pha Tat Luang

Vientiane's biggest annual festival is *boun pha tat luang*. Held around the city landmark and temple of Pha Tat Luang for several days over the full moon period in November, the colourful event includes music and dance, parades and night markets. The highlights, however, are the early morning alms-giving ceremony for hundreds of monks and an evening candle-lit procession around the glistening golden stupa.

Arts and Crafts

Laos boasts many highly skilled artisans in silversmithing, fibre arts, woodwork and ceramics. Visitors to the country can enjoy shopping for traditional and contemporary crafts in boutiques and night markets, particularly in Vientiane and Luang Prabang.

Above: Beautiful silk textiles are made on hand looms in many rural homes.

Above: Silk weaving in Laos is very much a living tradition and young people are still learning the art.

Weaving

Laos is renowned for some of the most highly skilled weavers in Asia. Villages across the country produce lengths of outstanding hand-woven silk to the most intricate designs. The beautiful fabric is made into *paa sin*, the traditional Lao skirt. *Paa sin* can be purchased in the morning markets of most towns but Vientiane also has an excellent choice of shops selling new and old collectable fabrics. Hill tribes in Luang Prabang also sell a range of distinctive cotton bags, clothing and bedding.

Above: The intricately patterned 'paa sin', or Lao sarong, is worn by all women at weddings and other special occasions.

Silverwork

Every elegant Lao lady dressed in her *paa sin* and silk blouse adds the finishing touches to her beauty with exquisitely crafted silver jewellery. Large bracelets and bangles, earrings and necklaces in modern and traditional designs can be bought in markets and boutiques. Old hill tribe silver jewellery is also available but quality pieces are increasingly hard to find.

Above: A potter in Baan Chan making a 'krok' with the help of his daughter.

Above: Must-buy items in Laos are pieces of beautifully crafted silver jewellery.

Pottery

In recent years Laos' traditional pottery production has gone into serious decline due to the import of cheaper, more durable plastic, enamel and factory-made ceramic ware from China. However, one village that has survived is Baan Chan, just across the river from Luang Prabang. Here, skilled potters produce high-fired jars used for brewing rice whisky, a pestle called a *krok* in which the spicy papaya salad, *tam mak hung,* is made, and various items for the tourist market.

Above: Clay for the pots is dug locally and thrown on hand-turned wheels.

Chapter 2: Vientiane

Pushed up against the Mekong River, Laos' capital city, Vientiane, is experiencing a renaissance. Once known for its distinctly sleepy atmosphere and laidback lifestyle, the city has been awoken by a youthful population, trade with neighbouring countries and a renewed sense of optimism.

Below and opposite: The promenade beside the Mekong River in Vientiane is a popular place for exercise and for enjoying the sunset. .

Today, the enchanting city welcomes visitors from around the world with a smile but signs of its history are plentiful. The colonial legacy of the French is now reduced to crumbling architectural gems, tree-lined avenues and crusty baguettes sold in the morning market. Communism, too, has left its mark with austere buildings, khaki uniforms, golden epaulets, reams of red tape and an economy in tatters. A visit to the Lao National History Museum, formerly known as the Lao Revolutionary Museum, on Samsenthai Road provides a fascinating place to get an overview of the country's past.

As the gateway to Laos, Vientiane is an endearing city with a rich history and valued cultural traditions, all enlivened by the buzz of modernity.

Patu Xai

Right and below: Patu Xai, or Victory Gate, dominates Lane Xang Avenue. A sign on Patu Xai states that construction was never completed 'due to the country's turbulent history. From a close distance it appears less than impressive, like a concrete monster.' In fact the huge edifice is worth a visit and there is a good view across the city from the top.

That Luang

Above: That Luang is considered the spiritual heart of Laos. Although legend says that the site had a temple as long ago as 300 B.C. construction of the golden stupa began in 1566 and was completed in 1641.

Left: In 2010, Vientiane commemorated 450 years as the capital of Laos by building a new temple beside That Luang.

Above: Beyond the outer wall of That Luang several golden Buddha images stand in the shade of a large bhodi tree.

Haw Phra Kaew

Right: Built in the 1550s, Haw Phra Kaew originally housed an Emerald Buddha image but when neighbouring Siam sacked Vientiane in 1778 it was stolen and taken to Thonburi, the then capital of Siam. The revered Buddha now resides in Wat Phra Kaew, Bangkok. The Haw Phra Kaew was also destroyed during the Siamese invasion and rebuilt by the French in the 1930s when they were the colonial power.

Above and left: Today, Haw Phra Kaew is a museum and has some extremely enigmatic bronze Buddha images on display around the outside of the main building. The image with the palms facing forward is Buddha's 'offering protection' position.

Vat Si Saket

This page: Vat Si Saket is one of the oldest and most atmospheric temples in Vientiane. The temple was built in 1818 and is one of the few to have survived an attack on Vientiane by the Siamese army a decade later. The temple's central 'sim' or ordination hall is surrounded by a walled cloister. In addition to rows of large Buddha images, recesses in the cloister walls house 6,840 silver and ceramic images.

Vat Si Muang

This page: *Vat Si Muang is one of Vientiane's smaller temples but is extremely popular with worshippers. Opposite the temple stallholders make and sell wax floral decorations to present as offerings.*

Vat Inpeng

Right and below: Located in the heart of Vientiane, Vat Inpeng features a stunning carved frontage, an ornate doorway and a colourful painted wall depicting the life of Buddha.

Lao National History Museum

Right: The Lao National History Museum, formerly known as the Lao Revolutionary Museum, on Samsenthai Road gives the visitor an overview of the country's past.

That Dam

Right: That Dam or the Black Stupa is a crumbling Vientiane landmark. Although today weeds and plants grow in the brickwork, local folklore says that it was once covered with gold. Legend also says that it is inhabited by a seven-headed snake, known as a 'naga', that protects Vientiane.

Around Vientiane

It is also worth venturing beyond the environs of the city. Day excursions include trips to the dam, Ang Nam Ngum, Phou Khao Khouay National Park and Xieng Kuan Buddha Park.

Xieng Kuan Buddha Park

A visit to this spectacular site created by one of Laos' great eccentrics, is essential. Located on the banks of the Mekong River, 25 km (15½ miles) south of the city and just 3 km (1¾ miles) from Friendship Bridge, the park was established in 1958 by Bounlua Sulilat. The shaman priest recruited local people to help realize his religious vision, one that combined elements of Buddhism with Hindu mythology. The park features a vast 50-m (164-ft) reclining Buddha and a host of other surreal and large-scale sculptures.

Opposite above and below:
Xieng Kuan Buddha Park has
over 200 Buddhist and Hindu
statues constructed using
concrete to portray Bounlua
Sulilat's vision of earth, heaven
and hell

Left: Work on the ornate
sculptures continued until 1975
when Bounlua fled to Thailand
following the Lao revolution. He
created another equally quirky
park in the Thai town of
Nong Khai.

Below: The peaceful park's most
dramatic image is the enormous
reclining Buddha.

Above: Vang Vieng's idyllic riverside setting and stunning karst scenery has ensured that it has become a destination for backpackers.

Right: The area is popular for kayaking and tubing. Visitors can also explore the many large caves not far from the town and enjoy cycling along a network of country tracks.

Vang Vieng

The setting is undeniably beautiful but despite its natural assets there's no sitting on the fence when it comes to opinions about Vang Vieng. To the backpacking fraternity it is simply heaven; for the true cultural traveller it is an example of how damaging tourism can be to local society. The once sleepy riverside town, perfectly located to break up the journey between Vientiane and Luang Prabang, is now overrun with cheap guesthouses and noisy bars. However, you can escape the hustle and bustle by hiring a bicycle and heading out of town to explore the peaceful countryside and quiet villages, all with a backdrop of stunning karst mountain scenery.

Below: Vang Vieng has a reputation as a party town with many bars and music venues open into the early hours.

Right: A good way to discover the surrounding area is to hire a boat and boatman to navigate the shallow river.

Chapter 3: Northern Laos

Mountainous and remote, northern Laos attracts eco-tourists, trekkers and cultural travellers. Here, bottle-green peaks stumble towards the horizon, an intricate web of rust-coloured trails clings to the hillsides, leading the adventurous off into a fantastic landscape inhabited by dozens of different hill tribes, and valley floors are carpeted with paddy fields.

For many, the highlight of northern Laos is the UNESCO World Heritage town of Luang Prabang, a charming and relaxed town set beside the Mekong River. The north is also the location of the mysterious Plain of Jars, one of the country's most fascinating archaeological sites.

Luang Prabang

A jewel-encrusted ring slipped over a slender finger of land at the confluence of the Mekong and Nam Khan Rivers, Luang Prabang is a city of many charms. Circled by mountains, the beautiful town has some of the most outstanding examples of regional architecture, a unique blend of local and European-style buildings constructed by the colonial powers during the 19th and 20th centuries. With its magnificent temples and continued adherence to local traditions, Luang Prabang is recognized as the seat of Lao culture. Acknowledging its importance to mankind, the town was designated a UNESCO World Heritage Site in 1995 and the old part of the town has benefited from a considerable amount of restoration work.

The World Heritage label has worked for and against Luang Prabang. It is no longer the sleepy Laotian town it once was. Yet despite its changes and an ever-increasing influx of tourists, Luang Prabang has managed to retain its dignity and charm. Visitors can explore ancient temples and vibrant markets, shop in chic boutiques, enjoy quiet moments of contemplation in cafés and savour local cuisine in al fresco riverfront restaurants.

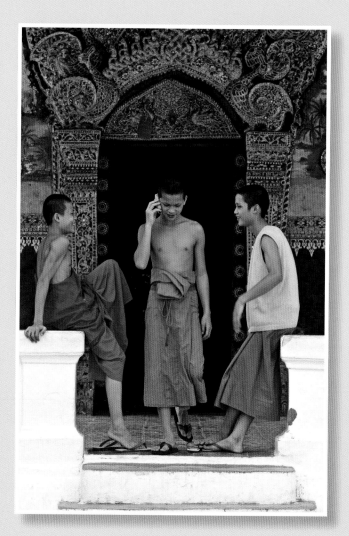

Above: *Many youngsters in Luang Prabang receive their education in the temples. Despite the monastic life, the temptations of the material world are hard to resist.*

Right: Every evening in Luang Prabang there is a vibrant night market selling a wide variety of colourful crafts and gifts, such as these hill tribe dolls. Many of the people selling their wares at the market are in fact from hill tribes and have benefited from the town's boom in tourism.

Left: Although not as spicy as Thai food, chillies are an essential ingredient in Lao cuisine. In the north they are dried in the sun and pounded into a spicy dip known as 'jao bong'.

Above: Ringed by rolling hills, the riverside town of Luang Prabang is best visited during the cooler months from November to February when the climate is pleasant and mornings crisp and fresh.

Tak Bat

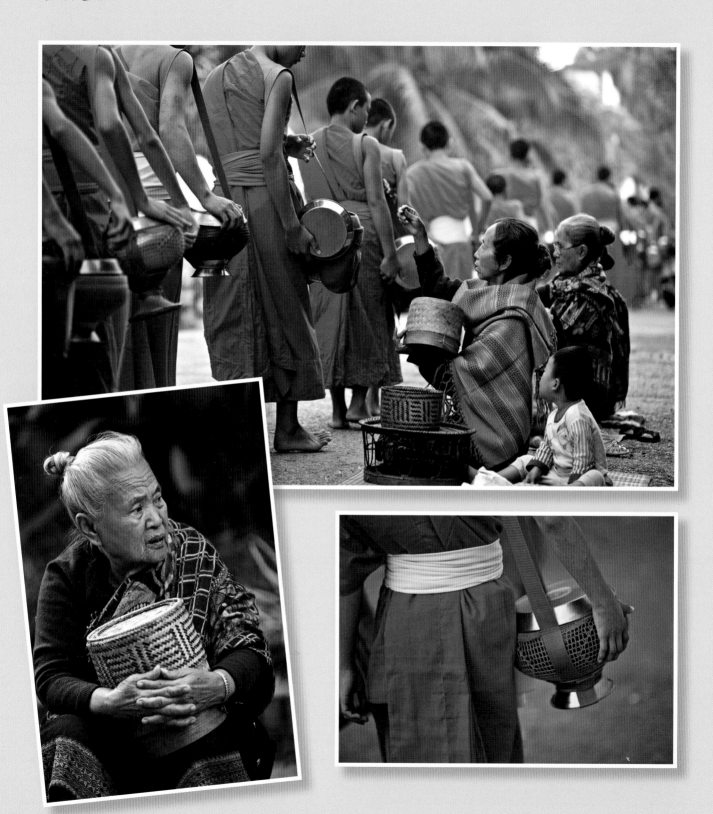

These pages: Rise early in Luang Prabang and visitors will witness the alms-giving tradition known as 'tak bat'. Each day at sunrise, locals prepare offerings of cooked rice and, kneeling on a mat, wait for the monks to emerge from the temples. At 5.30 a.m. the monks, resplendent in their orange robes, collect a small donation of rice from the faithful. By 6.00 a.m. the monks have returned to the temples to begin their duties.

Vat Haw Phra Bang

This page: Haw Phra Bang is a relatively new temple structure. Designed to house the Phra Bang, Luang Prabang's most revered Buddha image, construction began in 1963. During the Lao New Year, the golden image is ritually cleansed in a ceremony that attracts worshippers from near and far.

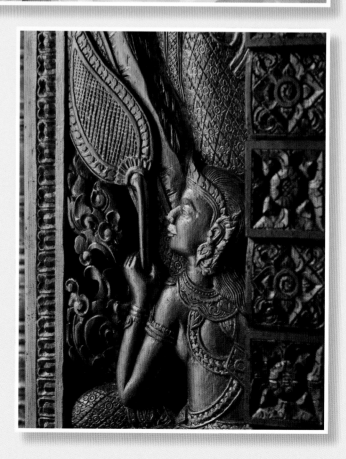

Phou Si

Above left: In the centre of Luang Prabang, Phou Si, a 100-m (328-ft) hill, offers views across the town. There are several temples on the hill with large Buddha images.

Above: At night the chedi at the top of mount Phou Si is illuminated.

Left: From the summit there is a clear view of the former palace and surrounding countryside.

Vat Xieng Thong

Above and above right: The temple features a wonderful mosaic of the tree of life, elaborate carvings and beautiful gold stencilled designs that recount stories from the Buddhist scripture. Vat Xieng Thong is one of the few temples in Luang Prabang that charges an entrance fee.

Right: Luang Prabang has over 30 splendid old temples, the most magnificent of which is Vat Xieng Thong. Built in the 1560s, the temple benefited from royal patronage until the revolution in 1975.

Vat Mai Suwannaphumaham

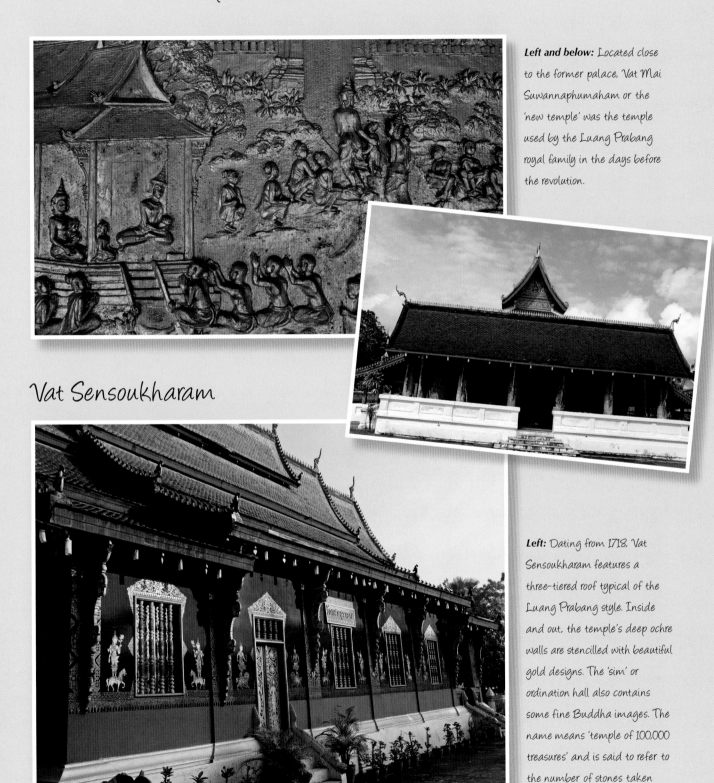

Left and below: Located close to the former palace, Vat Mai Suwannaphumaham or the 'new temple' was the temple used by the Luang Prabang royal family in the days before the revolution.

Vat Sensoukharam

Left: Dating from 1718, Vat Sensoukharam features a three-tiered roof typical of the Luang Prabang style. Inside and out, the temple's deep ochre walls are stencilled with beautiful gold designs. The 'sim' or ordination hall also contains some fine Buddha images. The name means 'temple of 100,000 treasures' and is said to refer to the number of stones taken from the Mekong to build it.

Morning Markets

Left: Luang Prabang's morning markets are fascinating places to explore. An array of local vegetables and specialities are available, along with fresh fish from the Mekong and wild food. Typically markets begin at daybreak.

Pak Ou

Below and right: Two hours upstream from Luang Prabang, the Pak Ou caves are two limestone chambers set in a steep cliff face. The reward for the strenuous climb is the sight of the dozens of Buddha images enshrined here. Along route boats often stop at Ban Xang Hai, a centre for distilling the infamous rice whiskey.

Oudom Xai

A bustling trade centre midway between Luang Prabang and Luang Nam Tha, Oudom Xai is surrounded by beautiful rolling hills. The area is also home to many Linten villages, an ethnic group renowned for their skills in weaving and silversmithing.

Far left: Vat Phouthad is located on a hill overlooking Oudom Xai and is a peaceful place to enjoy the sunset. An 18-m (59-ft) Buddha image stands in the middle of the temple grounds.

Left: An ethnic Akha Nuqui woman wearing her distinctive tribal jewellery. There are around 7,000 Akha Nuqui in northern Laos and 23 ethnic groups in the Oudom Xai area.

Below: Lush and fertile with rolling hills and valleys, Oudom Xai is a scenic province. Visitors can use the bustling provincial capital as a base to explore the area.

Luang Nam Tha

Located on the edge of the Nam Tha National Park, the town of Luang Nam Tha is an excellent base for exploring the upper north. There are many hill tribes in the area including Linten and Akha. The town itself is a sleepy hamlet with a colourful market and good restaurants and bars in which to relax and share tales after an inspiring day's trek.

Below and right: *Visitors to Luang Nam Tha can enjoy an early breakfast of 'foe' in the morning market before spending a rewarding day exploring hill tribe villages in the surrounding countryside.*

Left: *Akha villages are usually a collection of simple thatched roof homes that cling to the upper reaches of Luang Nam Tha's mountainous landscape.*

Right: Luang Nam Tha attracts eco-tourists who want to discover hill tribes such as this Akha woman (right) and Tai Dam (far right). Other ethnic groups in the area include Hmong, Kamu, Lahu and the Linten.

Above: A newly built chedi or stupa on a hill overlooking Luang Nam Tha is a good vantage point for surveying the town and valley below. The golden chedi was constructed in 2009 and is reached by a steep road at the northern end of the town.

Muang Sing

Muang Sing in Laos' far northwestern corner, near the borders of Myanmar and China, is a good place to see some of the country's most colourful hill tribe people. The town itself is very small and doesn't have a great deal to offer beyond the bustle of the morning market but is a popular base for treks into the hills. Visitors will notice the influx of Chinese migrants and trucks with Chinese licence plates. The region is currently being exploited for its natural resources, such as timber which is all heading for China.

These pages: During the cool season, the valley floors around Muang Sing district are shrouded in mist. The town itself is small and quiet but makes an excellent base for trekking to hill tribe villages. There are many Akha in the area (shown left) who are easily identified due to their distinctive headgear. Many of the silver coins used to decorate the hats date from the French colonial era.

Phonsavan and the Plain of Jars

Phonsavan is the provincial capital of Xieng Khuang, a region that holds the unfortunate title of the most heavily bombed area in Laos. The chief attraction here is the Plain of Jars, the main site of which is located just five km (three miles) from the quiet market town.

Right: Phonsavan is an essential destination on any travel itinerary in Laos. Although the town itself is an ordinary provincial centre, it is surrounded by the mysterious Plain of Jars. There are three sites within easy reach of the town, all of which have an extensive collection of the stone jars but there are also many more minor sites in the area.

Above: As a result of the U.S. campaign to carpet bomb Laos during its war on Vietnam, many of the jars were damaged. Huge bomb craters are visible and when visiting the sites it is important to stick to pathways cleared by UXO teams as there is still a large amount of unexploded ordnance in the area.

Phongsali

Reached by a rough unsealed road, the far northern town of Phongsali has a character unlike any other town in Laos. The majority of the population in this intriguing mountain hamlet are *Phu Noi*, an ethnic group also found in Vietnam, where they are known as *Khoong*.

Above: *A remote mountain town ringed by mountains, Phongsali feels more like China than Laos.*

Right: *In the Phonsavan area, villagers use so-called 'bomb-boats' made from fuel tanks jettisoned by US. planes during bombing raids over Laos.*

Chapter 4: Central Laos

Bordered by the Mekong River to the west and Vietnam to the east, the landscape of central Laos includes an expansive floodplain covered with rice paddies and remote mountainous areas that contain seven National Biodiversity Conservation Areas. Visitors to the principal towns of Tha Khaek and Savannakhet can enjoy the faded charm of colonial-era architecture, fresh markets and Mekong sunsets.

Above: The central region of Laos is the country's 'rice bowl'.

Left: Towns in the region also have many examples of French colonial architecture.

Above: In Laos, most people buy fresh food from the market every day.

Right: Rice planting and harvesting in Laos are still done by hand. The backbreaking work involves uprooting seedlings from the nursery, gathering them together in bunches and replanting in rows in another paddy field.

Tha Khaek

In recent years, Khammouane Province has become increasingly popular with eco-tourists who come to explore the lakes, forests and spectacular limestone karst scenery. Located 580 km (360 miles) southeast of Vientiane, the provincial capital of Tha Khaek is now connected to Nakhom Phanom in Thailand via the third Friendship Bridge to be built. The town is a pleasant stopover before heading further south.

Above: The tree-lined streets and administrative buildings that are still used today are a legacy of the French rule.

Opposite: That Sikhottabong is located six kilometres (three and three-quarter miles) from Tha Khaek. The 30-m (98-ft) white and gold chedi here is believed to date from the sixth century. The temple is considered an important religious site and a three-day festival is held here every February.

Below right and left: Rice harvested from the plains around Tha Khaek is sold in the morning markets. The town is only a short distance from the Vietnamese border and many Vietnamese live here. In recent years, the town has benefited from increasing investment from Vietnam and Thailand.

Savannakhet

With a Friendship Bridge spanning the Mekong to Mukdahan in Thailand, Savannakhet is an increasingly important trade junction between Thailand and Vietnam. The province is also the most highly populated area of Laos. Affectionately referred to as Savan, the town has many beautiful old French buildings dating from the colonial period which are in need of restoration. On the outskirts of the town, the Savan Vegas casino tempts Thai gamblers to the tables.

This page: The old quarter of Savannakhet has some fine examples of French colonial building but after years of neglect many are in a state of disrepair.

This page: *The large morning market at Savannakhet sells almost anything you could need, including fresh produce and sticky rice baskets. There is seemingly no limit to the amount of shopping that can be carried on a motorcycle.*

Above: A detail of the wall of Vat Sainyphum.

These pages: Located a short distance from the Mekong River, Vat Sainyphum is the largest and most colourful temple in Savannakhet. Although there has been a temple on the site since the 1500s, most of the buildings here date from the 19th century. The temple also includes a school for teaching novice monks.

Chapter 5: Southern Laos

In the south, the Mekong River breaks away from the Thai border and passes through the market town of Pakse, then carves the intriguing landscape into 4,000 islands before continuing its journey into Cambodia. The region also embraces the Bolaven Plateau, the home of Lao coffee.

Right: A massive hilltop Buddha image overlooks Don Khong, the largest of the 4,000 Islands.

Above: The 4,000 Islands is one on Laos' most beautiful areas but also one of its most popular with backpackers. The island of Don Det attracts droves of travellers who enjoy cheap riverside accommodation and days lazing in the sun. Fortunately there are several quieter islands to explore which are still unspoilt.

Pakse

The largest town in Champasak Province, Pakse sits at the confluence of the Mekong River and the Se Don, from which it gets its name (Pakse means 'mouth of the river Se'). The town is home to the biggest fresh market in Laos as well as a daily riverfront pig market where locals haggle with Vietnamese traders for the best price for their livestock. Peaceful evenings in Pakse can be spent dining on floating restaurants as the sun sinks into the Mekong.

Left: Vat Luang in the centre of Pakse is also the location of a monastic college. The ashes of a former Lao prime minister are entombed here.

Above: Pakse is renowned for Dao Heung, the biggest fresh market in Laos. Take the riverside road and you will also see a Vietnamese pig market, which operates every morning from daybreak.

Bolaven Plateau

Lying just east of Pakse, the expansive Bolaven Plateau's altitude and cool climate made it the location for coffee plantations during French rule. When Laos gained independence the industry went into decline but in recent years has enjoyed a revival. Today, hundreds of villagers tend coffee bushes and there are also several large commercial plantations, mainly around the town of Pakxong. Organic Pakxong coffee can be found for sale in the markets across Laos.

Below: Almost all villages in the area are involved in growing coffee beans. After harvest, the raw beans are laid out to dry in the sun before being sold on to roasters and suppliers. Although most of the coffee is low-quality Robusta and still sold within the country, in recent years more Arabica bushes have been planted and the improved quality means that exports are increasing.

Above: The orange cloth around the trees has been tied by monks in a ceremony to protect them from being cut down for timber. Once regarded as one of Southeast Asia's most untouched nations, Laos is now suffering from rampant legal and illegal logging.

This page: The Bolaven Plateau is an area of unique landscape between the Mekong River to the west and the Annamite Mountains to the east. The plateau features several rivers and many cascading waterfalls. In recent years, the area has begun to attract an increasing number of tourists keen to explore the landscape and ethnic villages on guided treks. A popular stopover is Tad Lo, a scenic hamlet set beside a multi-tiered waterfall. Due to the elevation of the Bolaven Plateau it enjoys a pleasant micro-climate but can be very chilly from November to February.

Champasak

The sleepy riverside town of Champasak draws visitors who come to see the nearby temple of Vat Phou. Located 12 km (7½ miles) from the town, the UNESCO World Heritage Temple dates from the sixth century but was a part of the Khmer Angkor Empire between the 10th and 13th centuries. As one of the most significant historical sites in Laos, it is an essential feature on any travel itinerary.

Above and opposite: *Vat Phou is Laos' most important religious site. The temple complex comprises six levels. The steep climb up to the top level of the temple ruins ensures a spectacular view across the surrounding area.*

Left: *Once at the top Lao visitors and other Buddhists make an offering of flowers, candles and incense at the shrine.*

Si Pan Don – 4,000 Islands

Just south of Champasak, the Mekong widens, creating an area of islands and sandbars know as Si Pan Don, the 4,000 Islands. Varying in size with the seasonal rise and fall of the Mekong, many are uninhabited. Larger islands such as Don Khong, Don Det and Don Khon are extremely popular with travellers. Don Khon is also the location of the famous Li Phi Falls.

Above and right: The southernmost islands of Don Det and Don Khon are connected by a bridge built by the French for a narrow gauge railway. Although the line has long since been removed, an old rusting train can still be seen there.

Below: On the 4,000 Islands, life moves forward at a slower pace but there are many interesting temples and villages to explore.

Above: The Li Phi Falls, also known as Tat Somphamit, are a series of violent rapids located on the western edge of Don Khon. The sight is particularly impressive at the height of the rainy season in September. The Li Phi Falls are used by local fishermen who risk life and limb building large wooden traps here, a considerable feat as the current is extremely powerful. In the waters further south, boats can be hired for trips to try to spot the endangered Irrawaddy Dolphin.

Left: Many of the waterways around the 4,000 Islands are more peaceful than the Li Phi Falls and can be explored by kayak. In the main stretches of the Mekong River, hundreds of fishermen can be seen laying nets or hauling in their catch.

Getting About

Getting around Laos can present travellers with a few challenges and discomforts, particularly if they intend to travel by road and off the beaten track. Advanced planning is important.

Most visitors to the country arrive at one of two airports, Wattay Airport and the main gateway to Laos, 4 km (2½ miles) east of Vientiane, or Luang Prabang Airport, 5 km (3 miles) from the centre of the UNESCO World Heritage town. On arrival, taxis or minivans are available to take travellers to their hotels for a fixed fee of US$6 and US$8 respectively. Pakse and Savannakhet also welcome international flights. Laos is served by a number of international flights with airlines that include its national carrier, Lao Airlines, as well as Bangkok Airways, Thai Airways and Vietnam Airlines. Domestic airports served by Lao Airlines include Phonsavan (Xien Khuang), Luang Nam Tha, Oudom Xai and Houei Xai, however, it is not uncommon for domestic flights to be delayed or cancelled if bookings are low. International and domestic flights often run at full capacity during the peak season between

Above: A 'jumbo' zips through the centre of Vientiane.

November and February and during the Lao New Year in April, so advanced booking is recommended.

Laos has several border crossings which can be used to enter the country. The most frequently used is the Friendship Bridge that connects Vientiane with Nong Khai in Thailand. The train from Thailand also crosses the short distance into Laos here, stopping on the outskirts of Vientiane. There are also Friendship Bridges connecting Mukdahan in Thailand to Savannakhet in Laos and Nakhon Phanom in Thailand to Tha Khaek in Laos. Backpackers also use border crossings with Vietnam and Cambodia.

Bus travel in Laos is cheap and popular and on the excellent main highway, Route 13, a comfortable and speedy journey if you choose a VIP coach. Advanced booking of your seat is recommended. Ordinary local buses stop frequently and can often break down. A good alternative is to hire a minivan and driver through a local tour company. Laos is a mountainous country and many roads are windy and steep. As with many developing countries, the condition

Above: A 'songtaew', literally 'two benches', is a popular and cheap method of transport in Laos.

of roads can be poor, ranging from unsealed main roads to rough red dirt trails that can be extremely dusty in the dry season and impassable in the rainy season. However, Laos continues to upgrade roads with grants from donor countries and the network is gradually improving. Traffic outside of the capital of Vientiane is extremely light. The standard of driving is extremely terrible and caution is advised. Erratic driving and overtaking with little regard for oncoming traffic are common, as is pulling out into a main road without looking. Roadside hazards include children playing, pigs, goats, chickens and farm vehicles.

With an extensive network of rivers, boats and ferries are a common way to travel. Several tour operators offer luxury cruises on the Mekong River. The most popular journeys are from Houei Xai to Luang Prabang and from Pakse to the Si Pan Don and back. The southern excursion is aboard the *Vat Phou*, an air-conditioned teak barge with 12 cabins. In the north, travellers board a purpose-built 34-m (112-ft) river barge, stopping overnight at a resort in Pak Beng.

The *tuk-tuk* or *jumbo*, a tuk-tuk with a motorcycle frontend, are good options for zipping around Vientiane and Luang Prabang but settle a price before beginning a journey. Drivers can also be hired for a day's sightseeing. A convenient way to travel around larger towns and in the countryside is by hiring a scooter or bicycle.

Above: Lao ladies when wearing their 'paa sin' sit side saddle on motorcycles.

Above: In rural Laos there is always room for one more.

Resources

Contacts

The following websites may provide useful information when organizing your trip to Laos.

Tourism information: www.tourismlaos.gov.la
Tours: www.greendiscoverylaos.com
Visa and travel advisory: www.bkklaoembassy.com
Things to do: www.visit-laos.com
Motorcycle hire: www.bike-rental-laos.com
Food and drink: www.tamarindlaos.com and www.beerlao.la

Airlines

Lao Airlines: www.laoairlines.com
Thai Airways: www.thaiairways.com
Bangkok Airways: www.bangkokair.com
Vietnam Airlines: www.vietnamairlines.com

Bibliography and Recommended Reading

Davidson, A. and P. Sing. 1995. *Traditional Recipes of Laos*. Prospect Books.

Davidson, A. 2000. *Fish and Fish Dishes of Laos*. Prospect Books.

Stuart-Fox, M. 1997. *A History of Laos*. Cambridge University Press.

Evans, G. and M. Osborne. 2010. *A Short History of Laos: The Land in Between*. Allen & Unwin.

Shippen, M. 2005. *Traditional Ceramics of South East Asia*. A&C Black.

Pholsena, V. and R. Banonyong. 2006. *Laos – From Buffer State to Crossroads?* Mekong Press.

Sutton, S., T. Page and L McGrath. 2011. *Laos: Legacy of a Secret*. Dewi Lewis Publishing.

Acknowledgements

Many thanks to Ponpailin Kaewduangdee, Madam Aong and Ivan Lewellen Scholte at the delightful Apsara Hotel in Luang Prabang, www.theapsara.com; Beer Lao and David Bowden.

About the Author

Mick Shippen is a freelance writer and photographer. Based in Thailand since 1997, he currently lives in Bangkok. Mick travels extensively throughout Asia conducting research for articles and taking photographs for local and international newspapers and magazines. A keen biker, he spends his spare time motorcycling and has toured extensively on and off-road in northern Thailand and Laos. He is the author of *The Traditional Ceramics of South East Asia*, as well as a contributing writer for the books *To Asia with Love*, *To Myanmar with Love* and *To Thailand with Love*. His images can been viewed at www.mickshippen.com

Index

ASIA BOOKS

Published and distributed in Thailand by Asia Books Co., Ltd
No. 65/66, 65/70, 7th Floor, Chamnan Phenjati Business Center, Rama 9 Road, Huaykwang, Bangkok 10320, Thailand
Tel. (66) 2-715-9000; Fax: (66) 2-715-9197; E-mail: information@asiabooks.com; www.asiabooks.com

First published in the United Kingdom in 2011 by John Beaufoy Publishing,
11 Blenheim Court, 316 Woodstock Road, Oxford OX2 7NS, England
www.johnbeaufoy.com

10 9 8 7 6 5 4 3 2 1

Great care has been taken to maintain the accuracy of the information contained in this work. However, neither the publishers nor the author can be held responsible for any consequences arising from the use of the information contained therein.

ISBN 978-1-906780-52-4

Designed by Glyn Bridgewater
Cartography by William Smuts
Project management by Rosemary Wilkinson

Printed and bound in Singapore by Tien Wah Press (Pte) Ltd.

Cover captions:
Back cover (left to right): *A boat ready for hire on the Mekong River; The scooter is the most popular form of transport; Close-up detail from Vat Sensoukharam, Luang Prabang; Fish are an important commodity in the Si Pan Don area.*

Front cover top (left to right): *Woman from the Akha hill tribe, Luang Nam Tha in northern Laos; 'Jumbos' are a good mode of transport for getting around Vientiane and Luang Prabang; The white and gold chedi of That Sikhottabong in central Laos; Monks on their early morning walk to collect donations of sticky rice.*
Front cover (centre): *The floodplain of central Laos is covered with rice paddies.*
Front cover (bottom): *Vat Sensoukharam, in the heart of Luang Prabang, northern Laos.*